DOWN HOME GIRLS

by

Allan Ishmael Young

Available from
FAIRLANE HOUSE
Division of
CANNON PUBLISHING COMPANY
3428 West Highland Place
Springfield, MO 65807
highlandplace@peoplepc.com

DOWN HOME GIRLS

No matter where a boy grows up, he will be faced with knowing many girls. Some will bring types of pleasures he never dreamed of, and some will simply be pains in the butt, to be avoided.

I always felt sorry for the girls. They were missing half the fun of being young. Of course, I guess their weapons were more subtle! And as time went on I was to find out just how subtle.

I probably had plenty of opportunities for extreme closeness with more than one girl, but was either too naïve, too scared, or too stupid to take advantage of it.

I have to admit that I never really had much of a "steady" girl friend, until I met the one who would become my wife—and not being from "down home," she is not in this book.

Herein are the girls I had to deal with all through grade school, high school—and sometimes before and beyond.

EMMA LOU WEATHERLY

As I turned to sneak unobtrusively out of the schoolroom to avoid having to explain my presence, she turned her head towards me, straightened up, and asked, "Is there something I can do for you?"

Completely taken aback, I tried to worm my way out of an embarrassing situation by being funny. Awkward, but funny.

"Yes, you can go to a movie with me Saturday night," I cockily blurted out, knowing she would laugh at me and refuse, so that I could make my escape.

But she didn't!

Being on the staff of the high school newspaper, I had formed the habit of quite often spending my last study period of the day over in the pressroom, which was located in the basement of one of the two elementary school buildings. Then, sometimes I would go upstairs to one of the grade school rooms for a visit. Helen Mullins, one of the girls with whom I had attended school most of my life, often served as a substitute teacher when the first grade teacher was absent. There weren't enough qualified teachers to take up the slack, what with the war and all, so a high school student would be asked to fill in—if nothing else, just to babysit the kids.

On this particular October day, after I had finished my projects in the pressroom, and, knowing that the first grade teacher was gone, I wandered up to her room, planning to talk to Helen. As I walked through the door, I saw immediately that the substitute teacher was not the one I expected to see. Bending over one of the students, with her back towards me, was a remarkably pretty girl with short dark hair. She was wearing a print dress of subdued patterns, with a close fitting bodice and flared skirt which showed off her feminine charms without being blatant. Her feet were encompassed in white anklets and brown loafers. When she turned around I recognized her as one who was a year behind me in school, but whom I had never met. She had the exceptionally fascinating name of Emma Lou.

"O. K.," she said, very nicely, in answer to my oh-so-stupid question, much to my surprisc, consternation and pleasure.

"Aren't you interested in what is on?" I asked, still afraid that I hadn't heard right.

"No," she smiled. "Do you want me to meet you there?"

"No," I said, "I'll pick you up. I can drive my dad's car. Just tell me when."

"The Saturday afternoon matinee usually breaks at around six, doesn't it? Anytime before that would be okay. Do you know where I live?"

"Yes. Why don't I come by at five, then we can stop in the drug store for something to eat or drink before the show?"

I went back down to the pressroom with mixed emotions. I had never really just come out and asked a girl for a date before. Oh, I went to school functions, sports events, and even to cast parties, after school plays and shows in which I had participated, with one girl or another—but this was a new experience for me.

When she came out of her house all prettied up in a nice skirt and sweater set, I was so delighted that I was momentarily apprehensive about telling her something I had planned to say. I had heard so many boys complain about girls wanting to do more than they could afford on dates, then being embarrassed by having to refuse. Although I had a good part time job, my resources for pleasurable spending were limited.

So, after telling her how nice she looked, and how happy I was that she had agreed to go to the movie with me, I very carefully explained to her just how much money I had on me. It was more than enough for the drugstore refreshments before and after the show, plus the show admission itself—but it certainly wasn't going to buy any steak dinners. I had eaten at home, and presumed she had, too.

She surprised and pleased me by saying she really appreciated me telling her that, and then said, "All I really want is to go somewhere with you. I don't expect to be wined, dined and entertained."

I had planned to spend a little time with her in the drugstore, which had a soda fountain, where we could get all kinds of ice cream concoctions and soft drinks, plus some types of sandwiches. This was also where all the students hung out when they were downtown.

"You know, Emma Lou," I said, "I've never walked into that drugstore with a girl on an official date before. All the school people are really going to be shocked to see me coming in with one as pretty as you. Besides, I have not mentioned our date to anyone, have you?"

"No, just my family," she answered, sweetly, and then her mischievous nature showed itself. "This is a very popular movie, so there will be a big crowd in the drugstore when we get there. Let's go in acting like we have been secret sweethearts forever, and really shock them!"

So that's why we went hand-swinging through the door, laughing, talking—and watching all the heads jerk around and the whispering start. We found a vacant small two-person booth in back, where we wouldn't be crowded by anyone, and sat there for half an hour, holding hands, with eyes for each other only, then left to walk down to the theater, still holding hands. By now, of course, our talking and laughing was more about the reaction of the other students and parents, and even some of the teachers who had seen us.

After the show we went back to the drugstore, where

several friends came over to talk to us, but we were still performing the same scenario, for the benefit of the friends. Except that by now I wasn't too interested in entertaining other people any more. It was getting to be for my pleasure, only. I didn't dare hope that Emma Lou felt the same way. On the way back to her home I found out.

Sliding over close to me in the car, she laid her head gently on my shoulder, and whispered, "I had fun tonight."

"Me too. I guess we put on quite a show."

"Even without that. That was fun, but I enjoyed us, too."

"I'm glad. Because that goes double for me."

"It's a little late," she said as we pulled up into the driveway of her folks' darkened house. "It looks like everyone's in bed. Maybe I'd better go on in."

I was a little disappointed that we were cutting a lovely evening short, but I complied with her wishes by opening the gate to their front yard and walking in with her. She reached for my hand just as we walked under a very large weeping willow.

"Uh, oh," I said, acting startled. "We're in trouble!"

"What's wrong?"

"This is a kissing tree," I explained, "and if a couple don't kiss when they are under it, it will fall on them!"

"Oh, my, we couldn't let that happen, now could we?" she said, turning towards me and sharing my embrace.

For the next few minutes we guaranteed that the old tree would never fall on us. We got way ahead of it, covering not only the present danger, but the past and future as well!

Over the next few months the other kids at school became accustomed to seeing us together, and pretty well ignored us. We shared no classes, so we could meet only before and after school, and at lunchtime. I had never been so happy in my life!

We never discussed anything serious, like even going steady, although I guess we could say we were. We just had a lot of fun, and some official dates. I thoroughly enjoyed the screwball things we did together, such as that day at the fairgrounds. As the school year was drawing to a close, and the weather became hot and humid, I found myself at some function there one afternoon, and she was there, too. Since her home wasn't too far away, I started walking there with her. Both of us were wet with perspiration, from our activities at the fairgrounds.

As we passed near one of the swimming holes nearby, she walked down to the riverbank and kicked off her sandals.

"Oh, no," I said.

"Oh, yes," she called back, as she jumped in, nice summer print dress and all!

So there was nothing for me to do but pull my shoes off, empty my pockets and follow her.

"Don't worry," she said, "our clothes will be dry by the time we get home!"

And she was right.

We had become so close that, like any other sixteen year old, I thought it would go on forever. But it didn't.

On the last weekend of school there occurred an annual event, the baccalaureate sermon for the graduating class, at one of the largest churches, and I was asked, or rather, told, to be an usher. Emma Lou was there, since her sister was graduating. She was always so very beautiful, even in a wet dress, but tonight, in a sheer white summer dress, showing off that dark brown hair, she was absolutely ravishing!

As I came by where she was sitting near the aisle, before the service started, she tugged at my sleeve.

"Will you take me home?" she asked, in her usual sweet way.

But did I detect an underlying negative note in her voice?

She hardly said anything at all, on the way home in the car. After we saw to it, for the thousandth time, that the kissing tree didn't fall on us, we stepped up on the porch.

"I won't see you any more," she said, almost matter-of-factly, as she looked away into the dark of the trees along the river.

"Why not?" I stammered, wondering what I had done wrong.

Here I had another whole year of high school, while she had two years. I had never given any thought at all to us not ever being us.

"My father has taken a job in a defense plant in Detroit," she said. "We are moving next week. He doesn't ever plan on coming back. He only waited this long so my sister could graduate."

"Then I'll come over and help you move. And we can certainly write to each other."

"No, I think we ought to say goodbye tonight. It's been great, and I’ve loved being with you these last few months, but we both know that we are too young to get serious. I'll never forget you, but time and distance change people-and it will us, too."

I knew she was right. Neither of us had ever used the word “love” before in discussing our relationship, and I knew we were too young to be even thinking of being “in love.” But, like her, I had loved being with her these last few months.

There are many partings in everyone's life, but none are any harder than the first. As we said goodbye that night, between kisses, for the last time, I knew that she was leaving a hole in my heart that could never be filled, and I was not at all ashamed to have my tears intermingled with hers.

For some time afterwards I rationalized my loss because of our parting my reminding myself that I still knew so little about Emma Lou. This had all been obliterated by my enjoying being with her. I could not even remember the color of her eyes. I knew she smoked, although she never did it around me. But I could still tell when she had been smoking. Many girls did, because the movies glamorized it. There was a small gap between her two front teeth, and the edges of the gap were slightly discolored—which I attributed to smoking. But I begin to realize that I did not know her favorite color, or food, or entertainment, or music. I guessed I didn’t really know her at all. But that didn’t stop me from thinking about her.

The Emma Lou story is my favorite, and, like all the others in this book, is absolutely true. But in order to tell the whole story of DOWN HOME GIRLS, we have to go back to the beginning.

HELEN FREELS

One day, at age four, I returned from playing outside to our coal company house in Kemmerer Gem, to be grabbed by one arm by my mother, while she beat me on the back with a switch. As I cried, trying to find out what I had done to deserve such a beating, she kept saying something about me being a bad boy. Finally, after the beating was over, and I sat crying in a corner with blood oozing out through my shirt, it came out that a little neighbor girl, Helen Freels, had come home without her panties, and told her mother that my friend Charles Kinser and I had taken them. There were several things wrong with that story. I hadn't seen Charles Kinser all day. I had been playing with another friend, Glen Raines, up at the entrance to Bailey's Holler, where we could throw rocks in the creek. Also, I had not seen Helen Freels, either. Besides, at age four, my little friends and I couldn't stand girls, and never played with them.

Besides that, what kick would a four-year-old get out of removing some little girls panties? I had two older sisters, lived in a small house with no privacy, and had seen bare bottoms a lot. Charles had one sister, and I presumed he felt the same as I did. I just felt sorry for girls because they had to sit down in the outhouse, while us macho boys could stand up. Also, even when the niece of some neighbors, who was about the age of my sister, nine or so, visited, and never wore panties, flouncing around our house, playing with my siblings, I just felt sorry for her, assuming she could not afford underwear.

About fifteen years later, after Navy service, when I was living, working, and attending school in Dayton

Ohio, I heard someone call my name while shopping downtown one Saturday morning. It turned out to be Helen Freels, whom I had not seen in years—now a tall, reasonably good-looking, chunky blond. She proceeded to practically beg me to come visit her at her home in the suburb of Drexel, where she lived with some relatives. I couldn't guess if it was me she wanted, or if she was just lonesome for a boy—or for an old friend. Still remembering the undeserved beating I had gotten because of her, I did not go—and never saw her again.

WILMA JEAN KINSER

Jean was the delightfully pretty younger sister of my friend Charles, who lived in the house next door to us in Kemmerer Gem. The most remarkable thing about our relationship was that we had no hang-ups about talking to each other. Our families shared an outside toilet, which the coal company had built on the creek bank between the two houses. It was still two toilets, with a dividing wall between them. One day I was in our side, when Jean entered on the other side. She had seen me go in, so she started a conversation—and we sat there, following the call of nature, while discussing many things. This really became a pattern. When I would see Jean go to the outhouse, I would go too, even if I had no real reason to be there. Our outhouse friendship went on for years, until my family moved away, when I was eight years old, and I lost track of Jean.

KEMMERER GEM SCHOOL GIRLS

When I started school at age five, I had to put up with a lot of girls, so I made the best of it. During my first year of school, one little girl, Roberta Pierce, sat in the seat just ahead of me. She was forevermore getting up on her knees in her seat, in order to see the blackboard. In that position, the constant holes in her panties showed. I just presumed it was because she sat on them, as all little girls in short skirts did, and wore them out. One other little girl, named Delsey Greene, who I remember as always wearing shiny black shoes, compared to the rough brown oxfords most girls wore, seemed to have a liking for me. She always showed up wherever I was on the playground. I do not know what ever happened to her or Roberta.

JOY OSBORNE

Joy was my age, and the youngest daughter of my parents' best friends, Jim and Maude Osborne, and I guess I knew her all our lives. They lived in St. Charles, and we visited them occasionally. Joy had a toy cat on wheels, which you could push the tail down on, and when you released it, the cat sped across the floor. I enjoyed doing that, because I had never had a mobile toy. Then one day she wanted me to go into a dark bedroom in their house. She was carrying two flashlights, which she shined through two peacock feathers, making two scary-looking eyes staring at me. We had a lot of fun with those props for years. As we got older, as teenagers, she wanted me to go to a Baptist Young Peoples Union meeting with her one night at her church. I went, and enjoyed it, although I knew few of the kids there.

After I started driving, and had to drive my mother to church in St. Charles quite often, I would not go to church, but would sit in the car and wait for my mother. One day it started to rain, and Joy came trotting down the street from her Sunday School, and slid in the front seat beside me. We had an enjoyable visit, but she kept telling me how she liked riding around in the rain. I knew what she wanted to do, but I knew also that my dad would be upset if he knew I was joy-riding. He had strict rules on the use of the car. I couldn't embarrass myself by telling Joy that, so I ignored her hints. I think that she got mad at me over it. But she could still be nice.

Later, I had to be at the St. Charles High School for something, and she caught up with me. We went for a stroll over across the street into the fenced ball field. Many high school kids were there.

When we were standing talking just inside the fence, the school's principal came charging up, and said, "Miss Osborne, you know I do not allow any necking on school property."

As she steered me back out into the street, I said, "We weren't necking."

She said, "That's what he calls just two people of the opposite sex just visiting. If there had been more than two of us, it would have been all right."

"We'll have to watch that in the future," I said.

And we did.

MARY LOU WOLIVER

As I said previously, when I was eight years old, we moved to Elk Knob, out in the country. The closest church to our place was the old Station Creek Baptist Church, and my mother made me go there to Sunday School early on. I was somewhat shy of all these strange kids, and sometimes my stuttering would come back. When the classes started, I was directed to a group of boys and girls my age in the back two rows of the church. There was a row of six or seven spiffily dressed little girls in the front seat, and a half-dozen or so little boys in the back seat.

The young lady teaching the class announced that she wanted everybody to say a Bible verse, and me being on the end of the seat, she pointed at me first. Between stutterings, I blurted out something that I had heard my mother say, "Blessed are the pure in heart, for they shall see God."

As she went down the two rows of kids, some had a verse; some didn't.

At the end of the session, as we were preparing to leave, the little girl in front of me turned in her seat. She was wearing a frilly white dress with socks to match, plus black patent-leather shoes. She had fire in her eyes.

"You took my Bible verse," she almost screamed. "If you ever do that again, I'm going to smack the pee out of you!"

And that was my introduction to Mary Lou Woliver. We never did become friends until we discovered each other on Facebook many years later. She too had moved to Dayton, and had married the future vice-president of the manufacturing company who employed her.

JANIE BRUNER

Her name was Janie Bruner, and she was in my grade at Elk Knob. She lived a short distance from us, on the same road, and began to come to our place after school and seeking me out to play catch. I complied as soon as my chores were finished, which was usually by the time she arrived. One evening when I threw the ball to her, she missed it, and it went into a ditch under some cedars. Soon she indicated she couldn't find it. When I walked up to help her look, she was sitting on a rock outcropping with her shirt unbuttoned, revealing a little pink brassiere. She usually wore very tight-fitting and revealing short shorts, but so did most girls in warm weather, away from school. Even in school, the girls wore such short skirts, and were so unladylike in their seats, that all we boys had to do was look around to be entertained by little pink panties all over the school room. I found it exciting, at my age, but I had two older sisters, so girls' figures were nothing new. But this was different. My naïve nature told me Janie just had trouble keeping her blouse fastened, so I just felt sorry for her. It wasn't until a couple of years later, when I got to know her better, that I began to think she was just letting me know she was growing up, that day.

MARGUERITE BELLAMY

Sometimes you can take on a school activity that isn't necessarily an undesirable activity, and turn it to your advantage. It might just be something nobody else wants to do.

Marguerite (they pronounced it "Margreet") Bellamy and I had been in quite a few school plays from third through fifth grades, and now we were in the sixth. One day we found out that the second grade teacher was putting on a stage play that involved almost all her kids, but needed an older boy and girl to play adults. All the seventh and eighth graders had run from the idea—but the teacher said it just wouldn't be the same with two second graders trying to look like adults.

"Let's do it," said Marguerite.

"Why not," says I.

So we jumped right in, playing Mr. and Mrs. Vinegar in a funny play about an old couple who were granted three wishes.

One morning, while they were still deciding what to wish for, Mr. Vinegar (me) woke up hungry, and said, "I wish I had a whole pan full of sausages."

So, immediately, right in front of him (me) there appeared a pan of sausages!

Of course, at this, Mrs. Vinegar (Marguerite) flew into a rage at him for wasting a wish, and shouted, "You and your sausages! I wish you had them hanging from your nose!"

And there the whole pan was, hanging from the nose of Mr. Vinegar (me). I won't tell you how we did that trick!

Then there was nothing the Vinegars could do but wish them off again—although Mrs. Vinegar (Marguerite) had second thoughts about it! All the kids, in the cast and in the audience, roared with laughter, and Marguerite and I were off and running. We were suddenly in great demand to play adults in many small children's plays for the next two years. It got us out of a lot of extra schoolwork, as well as some other undesirable activities—and we still received good grades.

Then, although we were never boyfriend/girlfriend, when we started to grow up, with the changes in our anatomy, I began to appreciate Marguerite over the other girls. In her basketball uniform, in grade school, then later in high school, she had all the right things in the right places. Not too thin, not too fat—just right. I liked being with her. Since her folks owned the grocery store where my parents shopped, I found many excuses to stop in and see her while she was working in the store.

Once during our high school years, I ran into Marguerite and her cousin in town after a movie, and they asked if I would like to share a cab with them to Woodway. When I said yes, we proceeded to board the only cab in the taxi parking place, with Marguerite cuddling up next to me in the back seat, hands on my thighs—with her cousin on the other side. We no more that got out of town than I realized the driver was skunk drunk. He was driving all over the road. Apparently Marguerite realized it too, because suddenly she had a death grip on my hand. I tapped the driver on the shoulder and told him to stop, that we were home. I didn't think he understood, but he stopped. I slid out of the back seat, opened the door on the driver's side, scooted the drunk over to the front passenger side of the seat, and drove the cab on to Woodway. We did not attempt to pay the driver. Marguerite told me later the cab was gone next morning.

HELEN MULLINS

I was sitting in a window at Elk Knob School during the lunch hour, writing something. Suddenly my concentration on my writing was broken by three girls who came walking around the corner of the building—two of them I knew, a very light blonde and a brunette, but walking between them was a new girl with soft-looking brown hair, whom I had not seen before.

The brunette, Betty Ray Stout, called up to me, "Would you like for Helen to come up there and sit with you? She said she would like to help you write!"

"Who is Helen?" I asked, while watching the girl in

the middle with more than idle curiosity.

"Her," said the blonde, Elizabeth Smith, pointing at the new one, who was now blushing profusely.

With that, I slid down from the window and confronted the three of them, saying, "I've never seen you before," to the new one.

"I just got here," she said. "I'm starting school here and I'm in the fifth grade."

"Good," I said, "so am I. My name is Ishmael Young."

"I know," she said, "my embarrassing friends here told me. My name is Helen Mullins."

She told me she had just moved from Bonny Blue coal camp where she had been attending school with various cousins of mine. Her father was a coal mine boss of some kind. I didn't think of her as being bubbly, outgoing or tomboyish, or even as having a pretty figure, as both Betty and Elizabeth, her two friends had, but there seemed to be some qualities about her in the openness of her manner, and the friendliness of her looks that really appealed to me. She had a very pretty face and exceptionally smooth skin.

After the lunch hour was over, when all the students had returned to their classrooms, I didn't see her anywhere. There was no other fifth grade room, so where could she be? Just then the teacher stood up and announced that she wanted to introduce a new student, and everyone turned to look past me towards the back of the room. Helen was sitting in the last seat in my row, with several empty seats in between. Being the tallest kid there, I had always sat in the last occupied seat back so I wouldn't block anyone's view of the blackboard.

Noting her embarrassment as the teacher and the other students looked at her like she was a prize cow at the fair, as soon as I could catch her eye, I winked at her. Later, after the students had settled into their routine, I stole a glance back at her again. She winked!

All's well, I thought.

We became friends, studied together. Could talk about anything, or anybody, and did. I learned a lot about girls from her, and I believe she learned about boys from me—just in discussions. She was high school valedictorian. I was editor of the school paper, but she should have been. She had all the ideas, and did much of the work. Good musician, she replaced Maidee Seagraves as our high school stage show musician, after Maidee graduated. Pleasant personality. Brainy, without hangups. Always had a mature look about her—physically and emotionally. Helen did not like sports or any physical activity, preferring to spend her leisure time at the piano. I saw her in shorts only once in all our friendship, and they were not very short. With that exceptionally smooth skin, to my knowledge she never had a pimple anywhere. We were always close, but I never thought of us as boyfriend/girlfriend. She dated several other guys, with one that lasted the longest. In perspective, I think knowledge of our relationship probably kept guys from asking her out.

This was brought out when we were sophomores, and Jack Collier, a big handsome senior football player, accosted me in the coach's room with, "I'm going to take Helen Mullins away from you," as he sprawled across a couple of seats.

"She ain't mine," I said. "You can have her. What can I do to help. Does she like you?"

When I told her about it, she said he had never approached her.

“Do you wish he had?” I asked.

“Might be interesting,” she said, raising an eyebrow.

The night before I was to leave for the Navy, I was in Pennington and ran into her. She was with her father, and I asked for a ride as far as Woodway with them. When we arrived at their house, her dad went in, while she lingered at the front gate with me. We chatted about nothing in particular. Suddenly, on impulse, I put my arms around her and gave her a long loving kiss, full on the lips—and there was a fantastic response.

“I’ve wanted to do that ever since fifth grade,” I said.

“Then why in the world didn’t you,” she answered, enthusiastically.

“I don’t know,” I said. “Afraid of falling in love with you, I guess. But I fell anyway.”

“Do you think that is a bad thing?” she asked.

“I’m lying,” I said.

“I know it,” she said.

But I wasn’t, and she knew that, too.

JAMES ALYCE LANINGHAM

Now let me tell you about my life as a thespian, with an unintentional humorous act. I had been in school plays all my student years, but when I started high school, they were putting on a blackface minstrel show. (Can't do that, now.) I was an "Endman," one of the funny men, who responds stupidly to the questions of the white "Interlocutor." (By my senior year I was the Interlocutor—in a white tux, no less.) There was a chorus of beautiful (or not) girls in evening dresses at the rear of the stage, and an occasional solo singer, duet or dance act interjected in the program.

She had the unlikely name of "James Alyce," the daughter of one of the two richest men in town—two brothers who operated the biggest coal company in the area, among other things. Everyone loved her, this little tomboy with the pageboy hair style. Her nickname had been "Squirt" in grade school, but I did not know her then. She was assigned to sing a song to me, and during rehearsals of her song I just stood there with my back to the seats, while I worked at recalling my lines—paying little attention to her.

One of the things I had to do in the show, playing the part of a jewel thief, was to race behind the chorus girls and remove their necklaces. I practiced this diligently with the cooperation of some of the girls, getting the hang of the clasps and fasteners. At a rehearsal, the director complimented me on being so adroit at it.

Then the twisted humor side of James Alyce showed up, when she said, loudly, “You ought to see him on bra straps!”

Then, after I got my wits about me, I brazenly said, “You ought to know!”

The first performance was going well—me in a tuxedo in blackface. Then James Alyce came out to sing her song, something called, "Tall Dark and Handsome, That's the Man for Me." This little tomboy had a high fashion hairdo, and was in dark brown makeup, clear down over her half-exposed breasts. She was an absolute knockout beauty! As she finished the lines of her song, she closed in on me, and I inadvertently took a step backward, and fell off the four-foot high stage! The audience howled.

The director said, “Leave it in, leave it in,” meaning she wanted me to fall off the stage at each performance. I did, with great trepidation. James Alyce sometimes accused me of upstaging her performance.

Good thing I didn't try Hollywood, I'd have been a cripple by age thirty!

ELIZABETH GILBERT

Late in summer I stopped at Hyden’s store on the way home from Pennington one night. Mrs. Hyden said her daughters were having a party in their living quarters behind the store, and I should go on back—so I did. All the kids seemed to be paired off, except for this beautiful girl sitting alone. We struck up a conversation—but soon I went on home. At school the following week one of the Hydens asked me why I didn’t like Elizabeth—that she liked me. I hadn’t even gotten her name. I said I had to get on home. I learned where she lived, so I called her from a pay phone to apologize for my abrupt departure. Then I couldn’t get her off my mind—Elizabeth Gilbert of Dryden looked like Lizabeth Scott, movie star. Strawberry blonde. Built like the proverbial brick outhouse. Every movement graceful and confident. Voice to match her looks. But she was two years older than I, out of school and working at a small restaurant in Dryden, and I never got the chance to know her very well.

Soon the summer was over, as marked by the Lee County Fair, and it was almost time for school to start. I had bugged Mr. Quinley, the Fair Secretary, years before for a job, and had been hired to take up tickets at the main gate. By the end of my first shift, I knew all the carnies, and was invited to all the shows and rides, at no cost.

At the end of my next shift, I was standing watching a carnival ride, when suddenly a hand grabbed my arm and a sweet voice said, "Want to ride that thing, Buddy?"

It was Elizabeth! Since I got to ride everything free, we proceeded to tackle all the rides on the fairgrounds. When the Ferris wheel stopped with us on top, I told her it wouldn't start again unless the couple on top kissed.

"Well, we do not want to be stuck up here forever, do we?" she said. And you know what? After a dozen or so kisses, the darn thing started going round again!

As we walked around the midway, I noticed a group of boys who seemed to be following us. I mentioned it to her, and she looked at them—then told me they were from Dryden. She asked if I minded her talking to them, and I said no. She came back a few minutes later and said that her old boyfriend was at the front gate, looking for her. When I asked if she wanted to go see him, she said she didn't want to upset me. I told her we were just riding a few rides—no obligation. She left with the group, and didn't come back. I ran into her at various places later, and she would tell me they were on-again off-again in the romance department.

EMMA PROVENCE

One day I was standing by the radiator outside Mrs. Carpenter's high school classroom waiting for her to come back from lunch. She usually went up to the Agricultural Building and had lunch with her husband. I don't mind admitting that I was somewhat her "teacher's pet" because of my math ability. I could do problems in my head that others couldn't do on paper or the blackboard. We needed only two years of math to graduate, but I graduated with the equivalent of six.

Emma Provence, her sister Charlcy, Mary Lee Carpenter and one other girl came along and stopped to talk. My brother, a sophomore, came by and I introduced him. None of the girls believed he was my brother, because we looked so different. They were all laughing about what they thought was a ruse on my part. About this time Mrs. Carpenter came in and I went into her room.

"You have quite a following," she said, teasingly.

"They're really nice little girls," I said. "I like talking to them."

"You do know one is mine, don't you?" she asked.

"Of course," I said, then I added, "I'm thinking about asking one of them to the Press Banquet."

"Which one?" asked Mrs. Carpenter, following up on my statement, probably fearing that it was her own daughter.

"Emma," I said.

"But she moved away," she said.

"No, not Emma Lou Weatherly," I said. "Emma Provence. What do you think?"

Then I told her about my being rejected by the St. Charles girl, whom I had asked.

"I don't know," she said. "If it were Mary Lee I wouldn't let her go. We have told her no dating until she is sixteen. Most parents feel that way. Emma is a little older than the others. She is in the same grade as her sister and the others because of some kind of illness that delayed her starting school for a couple of years. But I don't believe she is sixteen yet. Have you and

Emma ever done anything together?"

"No, except when a school gang had a wiener roast and marshmallow toast at the old CCC camp at Jonesville, recently, where I sorta followed her around. But she is always with a bunch of girls, and they can't be split up."

"You might get another rejection, even if she wants to go," she said. "Especially if her folks feel like I do. Don't feel too bad if it happens."

"After what happened in St. Charles, my plan is to ask Emma. If she says yes, then I will follow her home and ask her folks myself. I have met her father. He worked with my dad at Kemmerer Gem. I will assure them that she will be safe with me. Besides, there will be two teachers, Miss Campbell and Miss Hobbs, at the banquet, also."

Mrs. Carpenter just stood there shaking her head. I began to visualize Emma's dad eyeballing me like I was a teenage rapist, or following us to Big Stone with a gun in his car.

But I still wanted to take someone who would show better than all the other girls at the banquet. She was the only girl at PHS then who fit that description.

I stewed about it for several days, dreading being humiliated by another rejection. Then I decided against it, only to wish I hadn't.

Home on leave from the Navy, I walked past her house and she and her sister ran out to insist that I stop in and allow them to shoot some pictures. Then she presented me with pictures of the two of them in two-piece swim suits. Then, when I casually asked how school was going, Emma shocked me by saying, "I think everybody in school is getting laid, except me!"

I left.

JOYCE KING

Joyce was a pretty but skinny girl, with grey eyes that were absolutely impenetrable. When you talked to her, she not only looked blank, but you felt that she was not even on the same planet you were on. The summer before our senior year, Joyce swam quite a bit with us at the old Woodway swimming hole, below the highway bridge. Her two-piece swim suit fit quite loosely. When she swung out over the pool on the cable swing, and spread her legs, she left very little to the imagination of the boys down below.

Jewel Lucas, our art director for the paper, came to me later and asked if I still hadn't found a date for the banquet. I think everybody in school knew about my earlier rejection by a St. Charles girl whom I had asked to go with me to the banquet.

When I said no, she said, "Why don't you ask Joyce. She would go."

Jewel and Joyce King were such close friends that they even dressed alike and kept identical hair-dos.

I said, "But Joyce has a boyfriend."

"That's the trouble," said Jewel, "he lives in Bristol, so she never gets to go to any school functions."

So I took Joyce, problem solved. It was pleasant, as platonic friendships go, and we all had a good time. I drove Dad's big black Nash "Bootlegger's Car," and Helen Mullins and her boy friend at the time, went with us. They warmed up the back seat, while Joyce and I carried on polite conversations in the front.

KATHRYN MINOR

Helen Mullin's closest friend was Kathryn Minor from "across the ridge," near Stickleyville. When the senior banquet rolled around, Helen, knowing that I was not tied down, asked me to join her and her boyfriend in a double date—mine being Kathryn, whom I hardly knew. If I would do it, Kathryn would spend the night with Helen. Of course again, I had a car. Reluctantly, I agreed—really preferring to go to the banquet alone. The first time Kathryn and I had a few seconds alone, she told me I was not to consider this a romantic date, because she had a boyfriend in the Army. Fine with me. After the dinner, Helen suggested we drive to the top of the ridge. Under any other circumstances that would have been great with me. You could park right where the highway crossed Wallins Ridge, and look out over the fog-bound moonlit valley below. Wonderful place to take your favorite girl. But this night, while Helen and her guy were warming up the back seat, my date and I just sat there. I was glad when it was time to go home. The next school day, Helen accosted me on the front walk.

"You disappointed us Friday night," Helen said. "Kathryn said you had a reputation as liking girls, but she thought you were a dud."

"I do like girls," I said, somewhat disturbed. "Just not all girls. Besides, she told me right up front to not expect anything, since she had a boyfriend in the Army."

"And you believed her?" said Helen "Maybe she was just playing hard to get."

"I don't play games," I said. "I tend to take everybody at face value. What they tell me, I believe."

"Well, you missed an opportunity," said Helen. "She wanted more, and really expected it from you. We talked about it all night. I think this was really her first date. The boyfriend is just a figment of her imagination."

"Not my problem," I said. "You are my best friend. Just don't ask me out on any more double dates."

DORIS JEAN JESSEE

I had gone into the boys' rest room to wash off my makeup after appearing in a musical. When I came out, everyone had pretty much left. Hearing a strange noise in one of the classrooms, I went in to investigate. Doris Jean was sitting in one of the seats, crying. Big tears were rolling down her face, washing off the heavy makeup she had applied for her appearance in the chorus. All the girls were made up that way. I handed her my handkerchief. She stood up, wiped her eyes and face, and fell into my arms—starting in sobbing all over again. I held her close for a while, then asked her what was wrong.

"It's my folks," she said. "They bawled me out for wearing this evening dress off-the-shoulder. Said it was too revealing. Do you think it is?"

With that she pulled the shoulder straps down over her biceps, baring her startlingly smooth shoulders, as well as the beginning of the indentation between her breasts.

Then I remembered her boyfriend once telling me that Doris disliked wearing a bra, and how much he enjoyed the natural feel of her breasts against his chest—although they were both wearing shirts. Obviously she had none on under this evening dress.

"No, I don't think so," I said. "You don't look any different than most of the other girls. If anything, even more beautiful."

"My sister wore this dress last year like this," she said, stopping crying, "and they didn't criticize her."

Well, she doesn't have charms quite the size of yours, I thought.

But I had to admit to myself that breasts had never held that much fascination for me. I was a "leg man," and accustomed to admiring girls' legs every chance I got. And that was plenty, considering the shortness of skirts during those years.

"Everyone's gone, Doris," I said. "We'd better scoot, too."

"Will you take me home?" she asked.

"Sure," I said, realizing she lived a very short distance from the school, but too far to walk in a long evening gown. "I'm going to the cast party. It's at a house right across the street from the school. Want to come along?"

"I'd love to," she said, her eyes getting brighter. "Can I go in the rest room and clean up a bit first?"

So soon we were entering the house across the way, with her hanging onto me for dear life—smiling and jabbering all the while. She stayed in the living room, where Smith Warner, the popular local piano player for such parties, was holding sway, while I went into the kitchen to get us some refreshments. When I returned, she and her boy friend, who apparently had just arrived, were in a whispered conversation in a corner. Then they were in each other's arms, kissing. I retreated to the kitchen again, and fell into conversation with others. After killing time for half an hour or so, I returned to the living room, to see them going out the door, hand in hand.

Then I woke up to my suspicions, which I had all along. I don't think Doris had even talked to her folks. She and her boy friend had quarreled, and he had left the school without her. I had conveniently brought her to where he was going to be, although I don't think either of them knew it. Oh well, another romance saved.

RUTH PARSONS

"Have you guys noticed that Ruth Parsons has the best legs in school?"

The question came from Bobby Billings, a junior when I was a senior. Bobby's dad ran an auto repair shop near the school, and sometimes a few friends and I would go down there and eat our sandwiches—with a bottle of pop from their pop machine—while we pitched horseshoes out back in an alley. And usually our talk turned to girls—and legs.

"Just look at her sometimes," he went on. "Perfectly proportioned legs, and she is not an athlete. I first noticed them when I saw her in church, all dressed up in fancy shoes, a hat, and a pretty summer dress."

Later that afternoon I found Ruth sitting across from me in a classroom, and Bobby was right. With the short skirt she was wearing revealing about half her thighs, even though she had her legs crossed demurely, I was amazed and pleased at the shapeliness of her legs. Funny how I had attended high school with her for over three years and had never noticed. But then again, we boys were more interested in how much of a girl we could see, than how great she looked.

Suddenly she caught me off guard when she whispered, "Why are you staring at me?"

"I'm not staring," I whispered back. "I'm admiring."

She smiled, and turned back to studying her book.

A few days later she came into the Press Room to help put the paper together, as many students, not officially on the staff, would do on the day we assembled it. She sat down on an empty chair next to me, as we all surrounded the large table on which we worked. When I dropped my hands down under the table, she slipped her right hand into my left, keeping them under the table.

A little later, when someone was discussing school surprises, I said, "And some of them are most pleasant surprises," as I raised our joined hands above the table.

She seemed slightly embarrassed, as the others smiled or laughed, but she did not extract her hand from mine.

The following Saturday I was in Pennington without a car, so I proceeded to hike out to the edge of town, where I knew I could hitch a ride if someone came along who knew me. It usually happened. As I passed in front of the Parsons' house, she came out on the porch. I stopped to talk, and was invited to join her in the porch swing. As we sat there, chatting about nothing in particular, swinging back and forth, the chain on my side of the swing broke. Suddenly I was sprawled on the floor of the porch, with Ruth on top of me—her skirt up to her waist. She quickly recovered, jumped up, and even offered to help me up. She apologized profusely for the greasy swing chain putting a stain on my white polo shirt, as I climbed on a chair, and hooked the chain back by a less worn link, and leveled it up. I assured her it was not a problem.

Then, as I left later, she got the giggles—and I joined in.

"That would have been funny, if someone had seen it," she said.

"Well we saw it. It was funny. I'm just glad you didn't get hurt," I said. "But we made a memory today, for me, anyway."

"Me too," she smiled.

MAIDEE SEAGRAVES

I tended to be attracted to older girls, and sometimes they to me. When I was a sophomore I had a driver's license. I found myself with MAIDEE SEAGRAVES, who was a year ahead of me in age, but several more years in boy/girl knowledge. She was tall, blond, beautiful—looked like a teenage Lauren Bacall, and I was in awe of her. Good musician, played for our minstrel shows. In one, I was asked to sing "Pistol Packin' Mama," while dancing around wearing big shoes on the wrong feet. I was very concerned about my singing, until Maidee said not to worry—just to sing and she would follow me on the piano. It worked out well. After that musical, I found her waiting for me. I drove her home—in a roundabout way, per her request. Maidee had very thin lips for a girl, but she certainly knew what to do with them! I knew much more about what to do when with a girl after that night.

Years later I was in Radford to visit a girl at the college there. As I walked up to the college quadrangle from the town itself, I met Maidee and some other students. As we stopped to talk, I leaned one hand against a street-side building. Maidee worked her way around to cuddle under my arm. As it turned out, based on my relationship with the girl I had come to see, I should have pursued further cuddling with Maidee.

REBECCA FRY

That year REBECCA FRY, a senior, who, with her sister, Virginia, sang wonderful duets in the musicals, started hanging around me at rehearsals. Rebecca was a beautiful girl, not too tall, slender, with sparkling brown eyes, not too much around the top, but nice legs. Once she wanted me to go outside with her from a rehearsal, practically dragging me by the hand.

My sister, Stella, also a senior, yelled, "Where you taking my big brother, Rebecca?"

I was over six feet already, so she called me that—probably hoping people might think I was the oldest.

Rebecca called back, "I'm going to spank him if he doesn't do what I want him to."

Then came the most embarrassing moment of my school years—with Rebecca. It was after one of the musical performances, when everybody was leaving the auditorium, which was on the second floor. Rebecca, having been in the show, as I had been also, was wearing a beautiful floor-length evening dress. She and I were heading for a cast party down the street a ways. About halfway down the stairs, as I was walking behind her, the hem of her dress was spreading out over the step behind her, and I stepped on it.

At this moment the crowd stopped moving, and Rebecca screamed, "Ishmael!"

I looked down. She had taken a step backwards up to the step above the one on which I was standing. Her dress, with my big feet on the tail of it, separated at the waist, the skirt falling to the floor, leaving Rebecca standing there in the top of her dress and her panties. She reached down and lifted the skirt back in place, but I was every color of the rainbow. When I drove her home to change clothes, she just laughingly kicked her skirt off in the car, and sat there in her underwear, legs exposed. I made no untoward moves. I had done enough for one evening.

I wondered what her parents thought of her coming home with her skirt in her hand, but maybe she slipped it back on before entering the house. Soon she returned wearing a skirt and blouse, and we proceeded on to the party.

DEXAL LASTER

An interesting name! A year my junior, she was in a first aid course with me, taught by Miss Rasnic my senior year. When it came time for hands-on practice of artificial respiration, this tall, beautiful natural blond, from down the country somewhere, plopped down in a prone position on the floor, signaling for me to treat her as a victim. So here I am, astride one of the most attractive thighs in the school, with my right knee shoved up between her legs, massaging the nicest set of ribs I had ever touched. Being ticklish, she giggled, but Miss Rasnic complimented me on being technically correct in what I was doing. I felt like telling her that it was just on the outside. Then Dexal pointed for me to become the victim, while she practiced her technique as a rescuer. I think she was trying to tickle me, too, but

I've never been ticklish, anywhere.

I kept thinking, *Where has this girl been? Why didn't I invite her to the press banquet—or somewhere?* I had to admit that until that day, I didn't know she existed. And here I was leaving for the Navy soon. Oh well, c'est la vie!

JEWEL LUCAS

She was a good friend, pretty, and well-built, but seemed to have a permanent boyfriend—with whom she fought a lot. She and Joyce King did a tap dancing duet in most of our musicals. The boys in the shows couldn't keep their eyes off their skimpy costumes. Jewel was the art director for our school paper, and once when the Snoop column editor put in something about me having a crush on Jewel, which was not true, Jewel blew up. Didn't want her name in that column. I gently pointed out that the item was not about her, but about me, and I was the one to be offended. She cooled down, and apologized. We stayed friends, but no closer than that.

MARY HELEN ROBBINS

She lived right on top of Wallins Ridge. She was a pretty, vivacious girl, who played basketball at Elk Knob grade school and Pennington high school. I have always been wary of girl jocks, but she did not fit the mold. She was very feminine, but with an outgoing personality. Even though I had a teenage crush on her, the location of her home made her almost un-accessible to me. But then, maybe she would not have liked me anyway. That's my rationalizing defense mechanism.

HELEN STANLEY

She also lived high on Wallins Ridge. Helen was a year younger than I was, but I still had a slight crush on her while still in grade school. She too played basketball at both of our schools—and projected an easy-going grace in her personality as well as her movements. She had big but shapely legs, which her basketball uniform emphasized blatantly.

ROSE WADDELL

At the Kemmerer Gem school every once in a while they held a fund-raising box supper, in which the girls brought fancy wrapped boxes containing food, and the boys bid on them, getting the chance to eat with the girl whose box they bought. But the festivities were more than that. When I was about fourteen, and we still went to Kemmerer Gem sometimes, the box supper had turned into quite an affair—with booths, skits, games. In a fortune-telling booth were the Waddell sisters, alternating reading palms. The youngest one, Rose, was very pretty in the face, but her torso was severely deformed, leaving her walking stooped over. She read my palm for a dime, and she fascinated me. Afterwards, she sought me out, and we went to my dad's car and sat and chatted for a while. It was a warm evening, and I presume her gypsy costume was uncomfortable, because she pulled the skirt up high. I was shocked at how beautiful her legs were.

Eventually she asked me right out if I liked her. I replied that I would not have brought her to the car if I didn't. Then, when I told her flat out that I was amazed at how pretty her face was, and how much I admired those legs, she gave my hand a pleased squeeze, and declared we would be friends for life.

IRENE CHLEDA

Girls, what high school boy can understand them!

One day on the playground at the high school one of my friends suddenly said, "Look at the body on that!"

I looked around to see Irene, whom I had just met last summer. I had been on a cross-country hike on Big Hill when I came upon an elderly woman hoeing her garden in the yard of a small house beside the road. Straightening up with difficulty, she greeted me.

"I'm getting too old for this," she said, smiling.

"Nice garden, though," I said.

"I'm due a break," she said. "Want a cold drink?"

"Sure could use one," I said.

She called into the house, "Irene, bring some cold water for two people."

As we sat on the edge of a porch which ran clear across the front of the small house, a small blond, attractive girl came out and handed us each a cold glass. I thanked her, although she never looked directly at me, and she went back in the house.

"My grand daughter," said my hostess. "She is a little shy."

"I think I've seen her at high school," I said.

I finished my drink, thanked the lady, and continued my hike.

At the beginning of my junior year I was at some school affair at which this same little blonde sophomore showed up. Living way up on Big Hill, she didn't get to very many such gatherings—but this time she was spending the night with a friend. I joined them from time to time. We had fun, so the next day in school, I handed her a note saying how nice she looked the previous evening, and how much I enjoyed her company. The last note I would ever write to a girl! Within minutes, it seemed like almost everybody in school had read that note—and whoever hadn't, had heard about it. I was ragged to death. Later Irene found me alone on the steps to the press room.

"I made a mistake, didn't I?" she said.

"Well, at least you showed poor judgment, Irene," I answered. "That was meant to be private."

"Well, if that is the attitude you want to take," she said, self-righteously, I thought, "I don't want to be friends, anyway."

And she stalked away. I was convinced she was just too embarrassed and didn't know what else to do.

VIRGINIA WOLIVER

The first time I realized she existed was when the school bus jerkingly pulled away from its stop and the rear emergency exit door popped open—and a little girl fell out. Along with every other witness, I was shocked—but glad she was not hurt. She was a year behind me in school. I knew who she was, but we never became friends.

After Navy service, and a move to Dayton, I was back home for a visit, and ran into Virginia's sister. She told me Ginny, as she called her, had moved to Dayton, was living with relatives, and gave me her phone number. Later, on a bored Saturday afternoon, I decided to call her. She wanted me to come for a visit, that same evening. So I put on my royal blue blazer, navy blue pants, white shirt and tie, and set out—per her instructions on how to get there.

When I stepped off the bus, she was waiting—and I

was looking at a charming, well-dressed young woman—totally unlike the little girl I had known at Elk Knob. My whole being started to tingle.

When we arrived at the house of her relatives, I was ushered in and asked to sit awhile. I had a most pleasant visit with her relatives, who were very kind and solicitous of me. I didn't really notice, until I thought about it later, that Virginia was watching the clock occasionally. At some given point she suggested that we leave to go out to dinner. She had arranged for me to drive her relative's car.

When we got in the vehicle, she started giving directions, so I presumed she knew where she wanted to go. Soon we arrived at a large supper club out in the country. When I asked about it, she said this was her favorite place to go when dining out.

She picked a table to her liking and we had a very enjoyable dinner—all the while her charm and vivaciousness being showered on me to the utmost degree. She was warm, friendly and loving, and was making a great show of how glad she was that I was there. Considering that we had never been close, she was nice and openly attentive, almost to the point of embarrassment on my part.

I had noticed, upon our arrival, that she was looking around the dining room—observing her friends, I thought. If she comes here often, alone or with friends, she must know lots of these people. But the more openly friendly she was, the more concerned I became. At length, she suggested it was time to go home.

As we walked to the car she was very quiet, and the silence continued on the way home. When we approached a small roadside park, I flipped on a turn signal and eased off into it. There were no other cars there. I stopped the car and turned off the motor. I could almost feel her tighten up, wondering, perhaps, what my intentions were—what was I going to do next.

Very gently, I said, “Virginia,” as I touched her cheek and turned her face towards me.

Turning away, looking straight ahead through the windshield into the darkness, she replied, “Yes?”

I asked, “Was he there?”

With only the slightest quaver, she replied, “Yes, he was there, with his new girlfriend.”

“Do you think it worked?”

“I hope so,” she answered softly.

I started the car, and drove back to her home. I knew I had been used, but somehow I just didn’t mind.

HELEN HUFF

Helen never dressed sexily, you couldn’t tell what kind of figure she had under her clothes, but she always looked nice. Her typical clothing consisted of a skirt—short, as all the girls wore them—and an over-blouse, reaching almost to the hem of her skirt.

With Helen and me it was one of those casual things you really could not believe happened—and with no follow-up. She and I spent so much time studying together, especially during shared study halls, that some people thought we were a couple. Not true. But when I told her I was going to walk to the hospital during lunch time to visit a student friend who had been taken there the night before for an emergency appendectomy, she invited herself along. I led her from the school to the hospital by way of a shortcut, which meant crossing a small creek on stepping stones. When she saw it, she looked panic-stricken—then told me she couldn't be expected to cross that way.

I said, "Here, jump on my back."

She did that, wrapping her arms around my neck, and her bare legs around my waist. With her short skirt now slid up to her crotch, I was holding her on my back by my hands on her firmly solid thighs. She didn't seem to mind.

After our visit, when we came back to the creek again, I swooped her up in my arms and hopped across. In so doing, my hand accidentally went up under her skirt, gripping her bare thigh. When I put her down on the other side of the creek, that hand slid right on up her thigh—almost to "Miami," as the boys used to say. I had never heard the term "cop a feel" at the time, but in retrospect, I guess that was what I did—though accidentally. Helen didn't bat an eye, so I was not embarrassed either, and neither of us ever mentioned it later. Perhaps she enjoyed being touched. I always hoped so.

BETTY TRITT

Betty lived in a farmhouse across the river from Woodway with her father and an older and a younger sister. She was a year ahead of me in school, tall, blond and nice looking. I realized just how nice looking she was the first time she joined us in the swimming hole, wearing a yellow two-piece swim suit—all the right things in the right sizes and in the right places. One of my buddies tried to get me to double date with him and Betty's best friend once, and got mad at me for not doing so. I just figured I might be embarrassed because

Betty might be years ahead of me in the boy/girl department.

Then she and I wound up in church together.

I had gone to a revival meeting at the little Methodist Church in Woodway. I didn't care for church preaching, but I really liked church singing. That's why I was there this evening, planning to escape before the preaching started. Betty came in and sat by me. We engaged in a low whispering conversation about many things, until suddenly we realized the preaching had begun—so we sat quietly. Soon there was an "alter call," in which the church people try to get others to come forward to be "saved" and join the church.

I saw a woman in front of us looking around for a victim. She apparently settled on Betty and me—so here she came. I listened to her harangue about as long as I could—even when she asked if I would come forward if my "girlfriend" would.

Suddenly Betty said, "Oh, we're not married to each other. We are married to other people. We just came to church to see each other on the sly."

And she said it with a straight face. Our harasser almost fainted.

I said to Betty, "Ready to leave."

"Yes," she said, and we left the startled woman, hand-in-hand.

Once we got outside, I couldn't keep from laughing.

"That's a side of you I couldn't imagine, Betty," I said.

"It shut her up, didn't it?" she said. "C'mon, walk me home."

I begin to think I should see more of this girl, she could be fun. But I didn't.

MARY LOU SMITH

Mary Lou lived on a farm near Woodway. She was a pretty, well-built blond with nice legs, and the only girl I knew who wore white underwear. All the others wore pink. She was a year older than I was, at least as far as our grade level was concerned. Her eyes were slightly crossed, but to me it just gave her an exotic look. Whenever she looked at me, she was not looking straight into my own eyes .I sort of enjoyed it. One night she and I happened to catch an activity bus—a school bus which had hauled students to and from something going on at the school—back as far as Woodway. She let it be known that she disliked walking home alone that time of night. So, being the gentleman that I was, I volunteered to accompany her to her home. I enjoyed the walk, and I think she did, too. When we arrived at her house, she stepped up on the porch, telling me goodnight, and thanks for walking with her.

I said, "Is that all I get?"

She turned around and leapt off the porch into my arms, wrapping her arms and legs around me.

"I didn't know you wanted more!" she exclaimed, so we spent a lot of time saying goodnight a typical teenage way.

CORA EVELYN "CORKY" MATHEWS

Our freshman math teacher, Mr. Muncy, moved slow, talked slow, thought a lot—and got a few things wrong. On one of the first days of school, he called the name "Corky" Matthews—misreading "Cora." Well, the name stuck.

She was an average sized brunette with an enormous smile, and I never knew a girl with such a great sense of humor as Corky. Every thing was funny to her. We became great school friends over the years, and in our senior year she was a great contributor to the "Snoop" section of the school paper, in which she could use her sense of humor to write about school couples.

An example of her humor occurred when I approached her and Jewel Lucas, with Corky's best friend, Betty Waddell, in the hall one day.

Corky yelled to me, "I just heard a new joke!"

Jewel, looking embarrassed, because apparently it was her joke, said, "Don't tell him. You can tell Betty, but not him."

Betty said, "Why, she'll tell him jokes that she won't tell me!"

I was never alone with Corky, but it might have been fun.

SUE ROBINSON

Sue showed up at our school early my junior year, and was a year behind me. She was tall, pretty and overly friendly—at least to me. All the boys used to discuss her sexy walk—a sort of twisting side-to-side shuffle. I learned her father was a new owner of a truck mine, and they had just moved from some place in West Virginia. The family was renting the old Shelburne place just up the road about a mile from where I lived. Next thing I knew, after she learned we were practically neighbors, she was asking me to come visit her at her home. One evening I did. She spent the time playing piano for me and visiting—not much of a boy/girl date. I was completely bored, and later I suspected she was, also. I excused myself early, and hiked back down the road home. Even a girl's sexy walk can't make up for dullness—but she probably thought I was Mr. Dull, also.

BETTY GILBERT

When I was at Treasure Island Navy base in San Francisco Bay, on my way home to be discharged, I ran into Don Gilbert, of Dryden, with whom I had gone through the enlistment process originally. Don had shortened his boot camp time when he opted for Seabee duty. Now he was on his way to Bremerton, Washington, for a new assignment. He asked me to stop in at his home and tell his widowed mother that I had seen him, and that he was all right. A few days after my arrival home, I did just that.

That's when I learned that Don had a younger sister, just out of high school, and planning to attend Radford State Teacher's College, an all-girl's school, that fall. She and I suddenly decided to go to a movie in Big Stone Gap that evening.

Betty was small, no raving beauty, but she was still nice looking and a lot of fun. She seemed to prefer low-scooped peasant-type blouses, although she was not particularly well endowed in the upper story of her body. Her shoulders and chest were adorned with freckles. She had dishwater-grey hair, and nice legs—which she showed off by wearing her skirts a little shorter than most girls did. Still good to look at, from any angle.

After our movie, she asked me to join her at a marshmallow toast with a group of friends down along the river a couple of night hence. I sounded like fun, and most of my former school friends were gone, leaving me lonesome sometimes, so I went. We had a big fire, sang songs, played games. Had a good time, until some idiot threw a bottle in the fire. It exploded, and a piece of it cut one boy's cheek pretty bad. We raced him to the hospital for repairs, and most of the gang showed up there, too. Betty was pretty solicitous of him, to the point where it looked like they were a couple. I learned they had once been so. I went from the hospital directly home.

I ran into Betty a few days later in town, and she made me promise to take her to another movie on Sunday.

When we arrived back at her home, after the movie, the house was dark. So we agreed to park down by the pasture gate, and hike across the meadow to the house. About halfway across the field was a small brook. When we came to it, I gallantly swooped her up in my arms—being careful to avoid "copping a feel," and leapt over the stream. Then I just carried her all the way to the house.

After she opened the door to the screened-in porch, I deposited her on the floor—with my arms still around her. Then we heard a chuckle. All the porch lights went on!

Her family, plus a few visitors, had been assembled on the porch, when we drove up. Turning off the lights, they had watched our antics clear across the pasture and brook. Betty laughed along with them, but I was embarrassed.

Getting my wits about me, I finally blurted out, "It's a good thing we didn't do what I wanted to do out there in the pasture!"

A few days later Betty left for Radford.

Two or three weeks later, a friend of mine had to go spend a Saturday at the VA hospital in Roanoke, for tests. A buddy if his was going with him, and they asked me to go also. I told them I would like to go as far as Radford and spend the day there. I found Betty without any trouble, and we spent a delightful day together—having lunch at a downtown restaurant.

I told her I would come back to see her soon, which seemed to please her.

A few weeks later I decided to check out Virginia Polytechnic Institute as a possible college for me, and planned to drive up there—stopping at Radford on the way back. As I approached the campus quadrangle from the town, I met Helen Mullins and another girl coming in from the tennis courts.

"I bet you are here to see Betty," said Helen.

When I replied that I was, she told me I couldn't. Betty was confined to her room. I finally got it out of them—Betty was locked in for drinking. Further questioning showed that it was not unusual. Betty had succumbed to an ailment of which many Gilberts were addicted—a chemical dependency on alcohol.

The following week I received a letter from Betty. I said:

I'm sorry, but I can't see you any more. There will never be anyone for me but Harold.

I wondered who the hell Harold was!

FAYE HONEYCUTT

I had gone up to St. Charles on an errand for my father that summer day, and had remained late to visit friends. I knew a few of the high school students who were sons and daughters of friends of my folks. And of course I had relatives, boys and girls, in Bonny Blue, one of the coal camps.

During the course of my wanderings around the town, I ran into my cousin Howard, who said, "Remember my friend Darrell Honeycutt? I'm going down to a gathering at his house in Wagner Town. Want to come along?"

I remembered Darrell, a good-looking guy in his late teens, who seemed to be inseparable from Howard. Having nothing better to do, I agreed to go.

As we walked across a small footbridge to a house that sat between the railroad and the creek, I could see from a distance, even though it was almost dark, that there were several boys and girls on the front porch. As I was being introduced to Howard's friends, and greeting some that I already knew, I heard someone say "Hi" with such a sweet, female voice that I immediately hoped she was talking to me. I turned around and saw, sitting on the banister in the dusk being lighted by the rising moon, what was, without a doubt, the prettiest girl I had ever seen in my sixteen years!

I said "Hi," and just stood and looked at her, after awhile feeling like a total idiot. She was simply smiling at me, across the darkened porch, and I didn't know whether she was being derisive or whether she really liked my looks. Getting closer as someone turned on a porch light, I could see that she had long dark brown hair and exotic bright blue eyes, the kind you just fall in and swim around, and I immediately started swimming for my life. I had never noticed girls' eyes before—couldn't even remember the color of the eyes of most of the girls I knew. Bur hers were different. Suddenly feeling like a fool, I stumbled back across the porch to where Darrell and Howard were talking.

"Who is that?" I blurted out, looking back towards the girl.

"Oh, her? She's my kid sister, Faye," said Darrell. "I'm surprised you don't know her. She will be a senior this year, like you. And you seem to know a lot of these other girls, like Helen Carter and Joy Osborne, who are close friends of hers."

Feeling bolder, and armed with this knowledge, I tiptoed across the porch and sat down beside her on the railing.

She was chatting with somebody, but when she looked around at me, I said, "Good evening, Miss Honeycutt."

"My, aren't you the formal one, though, Mr. Young," she said in that musical voice that had entranced me earlier—even sweeter, now that it was directed at me.

"Apparently you know my name," I said. "I have to admit I had to ask your brother who you were."

"These girls told me," she said. "I had to ask them, too."

"Call me Ishmael," I said, "like the narrator in Moby Dick. I'll spell it if you like."

"No need, Ishmael," she said. "I can read, and I know it's also a Biblical name. As you know by now, I'm Faye. I won't tell you what my middle name is."

"I don't care," I said. "Your first name is the most beautiful I've ever heard, and it matches its owner—especially her eyes."

"Oh, my," she said, "such a line. How many girls

have you used that on? Whatever am I going to do with you?"

"I don't know any lines," I said. "I'm just stupid enough to blurt out my impressions and feelings. And as to what you are going to do with me, I hope it is a lot—whatever it is—and that it lasts a long time."

At this time some of her girl friends engaged her in conversations, and she turned her back on me—although I could see her twist her head around to look at me occasionally. I went home later knowing I was smitten—not thinking of my lost Emma Lou at all. I tried to pump Howard about her, but he seemed overly protective where she was concerned, and kept referring to her as a little kid. She didn't look like a kid to me. I did learn she worked in a drug store in St. Charles, and decided to make it a point to stop in there. The following Saturday I did so.

As I walked in she saw me and smiled, but before I could greet her, a male voice called to me to come over. It was Jim Myers' brother, Billy—known as Buddy, sitting at a small round ice cream table with two other boys I recognized from St. Charles high school. I sat down in the empty chair by them, while still watching Faye. She came over with a notepad and started asking what each of them wanted. Suddenly Buddy pulled her down on his knee, then put his arm around her while she took the orders. I was chagrined—apparently she was available to any old knee that was available.

But, I thought, *what the heck, this is not the first time I've been disappointed in a girl. But why her? I thought she was spotless.*

When she turned to me, and asked, "Did you want something, Ishmael?" I was burning.

"I did when I came in," I said, "but I don't now."
And I got up and bolted out the door.

A week later, I was in St. Charles again, when I ran into Joy Osborne. Her being my age, and the youngest daughter of my parents' one-time best friends, Jim and Maude, I had known Joy as long as I could remember. This evening she told me she was heading for a meeting of the Baptist Young People's Union at the local church. Suddenly she asked me if I would like to go along. When I hesitated, she said all they did was sing songs and play games. So I went with her.

The first person I saw when we entered the door to the church's basement meeting room was Faye. She was wearing a bright royal blue skirt with a white blouse, which made her blue eyes look even bluer. I could be wrong, but I think they got bigger when she saw me with Joy. We avoided each other all evening, me sticking close to Joy.

I saw no more of her after that evening—if anything I stayed away from places she might be, especially the St. Charles drug store. Soon the summer was over, as marked by the Lee County Fair, and it was almost time for school to start. At the end of my shift at the Fair on Saturday, its last day, I started wandering down the midway. Four girls, whom I had seen enter earlier—but the other ticket-taker had admitted them—accosted me. Included in those excited faces was one with swimmingly blue eyes and dark hair, easily recognizable anywhere—Faye!

After some polite conversation about what I was doing at the Fair, it came out that I had certain privileges—like free rides. Suddenly there was a chorus of voices telling me they liked rides—except that Faye's voice was noticeably absent.

"And you, Miss Honeycutt," I said, smiling at her, "I bet you are afraid of the rides."

"No," said one of the girls. "She is the one of us who will ride anything—the wilder the better."

"Then let's ride the swings," I said to her.

She smiled at me, and said, "Let's go. And I bet you throw up before I do!"

We rode many rides, and neither of us got sick. But when we rode the Ferris wheel, I didn't pull my ruse about kissing when the wheel stopped with us on top. Somehow I was afraid it might not work on her.

So I took her hand, saying, "Can I drive you home?"

"I had better rejoin my friends," she said, as we got off the last ride, neither of us having thrown up. "My folks will be expecting me to come home with them. I might have difficulty explaining you, if you take me home—even though I would like it."

"That's OK," I said. "I understand. I have protective parents, too. Will I see you again?"

"If you'd like," she said. "But what about Joy?"

"Joy and I are nothing," I said. "I've known her all my life, and that meeting at your church was the only time we have ever done anything together—besides play with her toys when we were toddlers. What about you and Buddy?"

"Me and who?"

"Buddy. Billy Myers. I was disturbed when you sat on his knee in the drugstore."

"I hope that's not why I never saw you anymore all summer! I hardly knew any of those boys. I was so shocked I didn't know what to do. Harry, the druggist, told me later I should have just gotten up and asked him to wait on the boys. It was inappropriate behavior—on the part of the boy and me."

"I'm sorry," I said, realizing that the summer might not have seemed so long, if I hadn't reacted negatively to the incident.

"I'm sorry for what I was thinking when I saw you with Joy, too," she said.

Soon we found her friends, and we parted. I watched them go out the gate, then floated on air back to my car.

As editor of the Monthly Splash, the high school newspaper, I looked forward to this most prestigious event of the year—the Press Banquet.

Where was Emma Lou, now that I needed her? I kept thinking. *Moved to Detroit, that's where.*

The girls were to wear evening dresses and we boys to wear suits, and meet in the dining room of the Monte Vista Hotel in Big Stone Gap, about twenty miles from Pennington. I had already decided to ask Faye, the prettiest girl in St. Charles, and everywhere else, for that matter, to go, getting the message to her through Miss Hobbs, the typing teacher, who spent mornings at Pennington High, then afternoons at St. Charles. Faye told Miss Hobbs she would like to go, but had to ask her folks—naturally. Then the next day she told Miss Hobbs her folks wouldn't let her go. I was literally heartsick. It never occurred to me to question it figuring most girls would consider it an impressive event to attend—even if they didn't like their date. Perhaps she didn't want to go, or didn't have an evening dress, or her folks wouldn't let her wear one, or it was too far from home. But no, it had to be they didn't want her to be with me.

I had wanted to take someone who was outstandingly beautiful, and who would outshine all the other girls at the banquet. Faye was the only girl I knew who fit that description. Then I realized I had done this wrong, and told Miss Hobbs so. I should have gone to Faye's house, asked her to go, then, if she indicated she wanted to, I should have asked her parents myself—telling them that there would be two teachers at the banquet.

But then Miss Hobbs told me that Faye's family had lost a younger brother, about ten years old, to a brain hemorrhage recently—so they had become very protective of their remaining two offspring. That shed a new light on the situation.

But I wasn't ready to give up on being friends with her. Right before graduation, I bought a dresser set for her, something I had learned my two sisters valued highly. Since she had no telephone, I just simply walked down to her house on Saturday carrying the gift. I met her father on the way, and he was civil—telling me hello. Faye met me at the door wearing a chenille housecoat. I had caught her before she had time to get dressed. She didn't seem embarrassed, but I was. I should have come later, but I had been afraid she might not be there. She accepted the gift graciously, and I left. I couldn't have been there more than five minutes.

Later I ran into her in St. Charles and she presented me with a billfold—which I am sure she had just bought. I left for the Navy a few days later, and did not contact her from there, or when I was home on leave, or after I was discharged.

Out of the Navy and living and working and in school in Dayton, I had come home to my room from work when my landlady called me to the phone. It was my sister.

"Grandma is dead," she said. "Can you come home? She had asked that her grandsons be pallbearers."

After getting the details of the funeral arrangements and schedules, I called the shop where I worked and the college and headed for the bus station. The wake was to be at my uncle's place in the Mayflower section of Bonny Blue.

Sometime during the course of the evening, while reading, I dozed off on the couch. I didn't know how long I slept—but I was awakened by being hit in the face by a pillow. I opened my eyes to see standing before me, with an impish, guilty grin on her face, the most beautiful girl I had ever seen. I tossed the pillow back at her. She caught it and sat down beside me. Faye!

Neither of us slept the rest of the night, and it passed so rapidly it seemed over almost instantly. The next day was the day of the funeral, so I had to go home and change clothes.

Faye was not coming to the funeral, but I agreed to come to her house that night.

The moon, high above the mountains, was extremely beautiful—and so was she. The evening, after I arrived at her house, was so full of happy talk, laughter and enjoyment. We were not even sitting together, or touching, and I kept thinking what a wonderful, vivacious, interesting girl she had always been and still was. I delighted in simply watching her. Suddenly it occurred to me that in all the time I had known her, and had been with her, I had never tried to kiss her. Maybe I thought it would be a violation of her arms-length demeanor.

Perhaps it's time to remedy that, I thought.

But the opportunity didn't present itself.

At this point, our visiting was disturbed by the front door opening, shedding some light from inside the house on the moonlit porch.

"Hi, Dad," said Faye.

I looked around to see her father standing there In the doorway dressed in only his pants, with the top of his underwear showing.

I started to greet him, but in the middle of it he said, "Get in the house, Faye!"

"Just a minute, Dad," she said.

"A minute is all you've got."

And he re-entered the house, hurling over his shoulder, "Don't be long. And you, young man, don't ever come back here again!"

"I better go, Faye," I said.

"Please don't. We can explain to him that we haven't done anything wrong. Or come back tomorrow," she said. "Maybe it will be all right then."

"I'm going back up north tomorrow."

"Please stay over another day," she pleaded, "here you have a new blue suit and all!"

I stepped over to her and held her close, and since she did not tilt her head back to look at me, I made no attempt to kiss her. I let her go and walked away towards the foot bridge that crossed the creek. In the middle of the bridge I turned around. She hadn't moved from the moonlit spot she was in, and I could almost see those ever-fascinating blue eyes full of tears. And even though I had no idea what my next development might be, I knew those eyes would haunt me forever.

The temptation to race back to her, and throw my arms around her and kiss her for the first time, was so great I had to bite my lip. Faye was a beautiful girl, and I really liked her—but I didn't like her well enough to fight her father for her. I kept going.

So there you have it—the girls I grew up with, and my fascination with eyes and legs, mostly legs. Some of the girls I knew until they died—and some I couldn't wait to get away from.

THE END

www.ingramcontent.com/pod-product-compliance
Ingram Content Group UK Ltd.
Pitfield, Milton Keynes, MK11 3LW, UK
UKHW041838200726
13854UKWH00003BA/1195